THIS BOOK BELONGS TO:

_____

The Wonderful World of Ice Cream

Mimi Jones

Dedicated to Kim D and MJ.

All rights reserved.
No part of this book may be reproduced in any form or by any means, electronic or mechanical, and no photocopying or recording, unless you have written permission from the author.

ISBN 978-1-958985-32-8

Text copyright © 2024 by Mimi Jones

www.joeysavestheday.com

A Mimi Book

Welcome to The Wonderful World of Ice Cream

Ice cream has its roots in ancient China, dating back to the Tang Dynasty (618-907 AD). From there, it made its way to the Middle East, where the Persians developed falooda. Eventually, it reached Europe and transformed into the modern ice cream we know today.

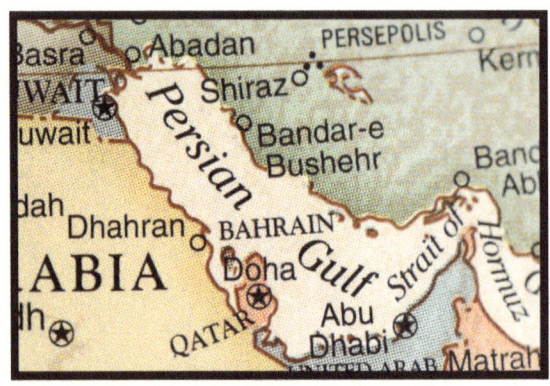

Falooda is a classic dessert that originates from Persia and South Asia, featuring a delightful combination of vermicelli, basil seeds, jelly, flavored syrups, and either milk or ice cream. Typically garnished with rose syrup, nuts, and a scoop of ice cream, it transforms into a refreshing and indulgent delight.

Some of the most favored ice cream flavors include vanilla, chocolate, mint chocolate chip, cookie dough, butter pecan, strawberry, and rocky road.

July is celebrated as National Ice Cream Month, with National Ice Cream Day occurring on the third Sunday of the month. This delightful tradition began in 1984 and remains a beloved celebration.

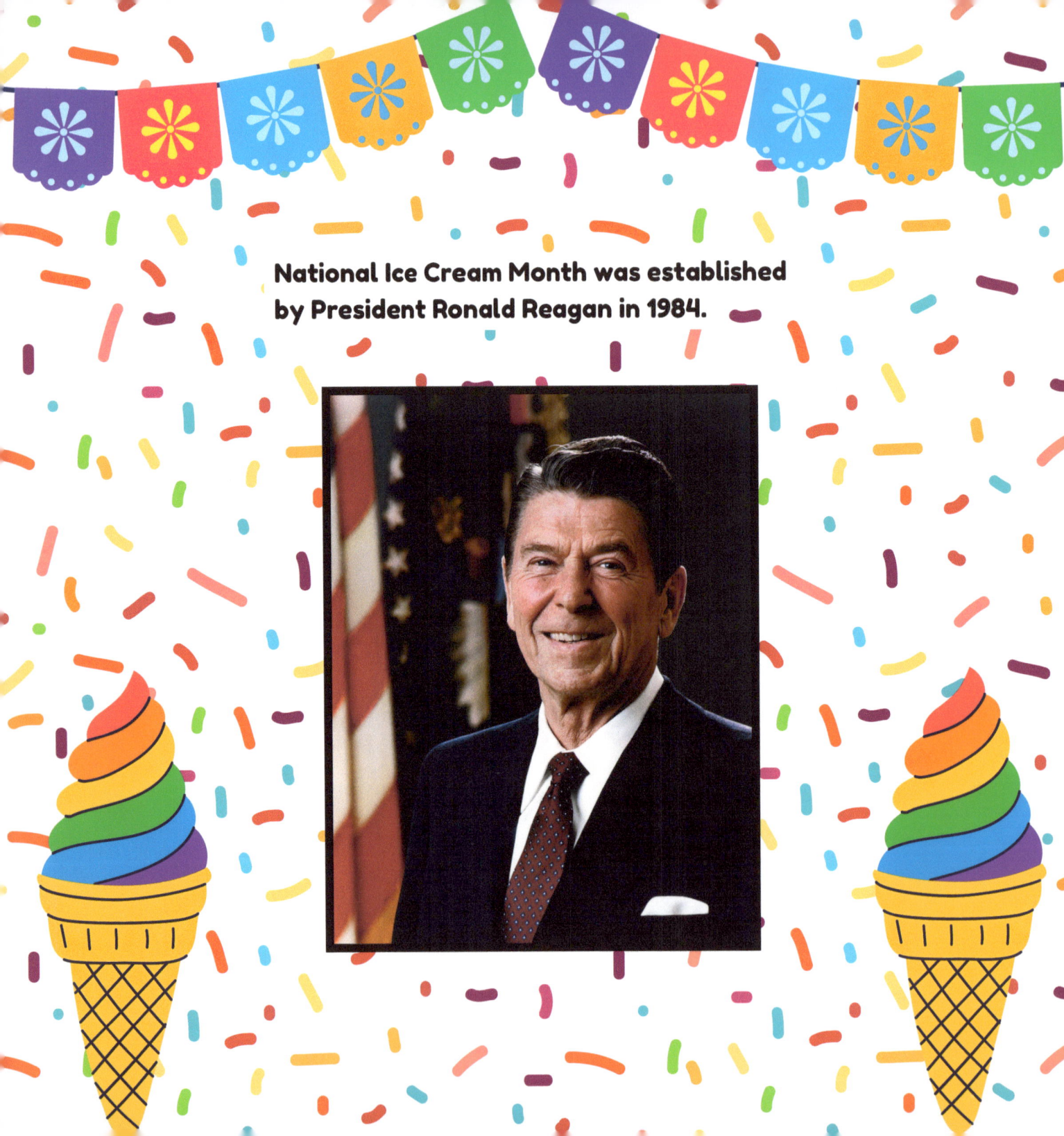

National Ice Cream Month was established by President Ronald Reagan in 1984.

Here are a few out-of-the-ordinary ice cream flavors: avocado, bacon, chili, garlic, and licorice.

In the late 18th century, ice cream arrived in the United States, with its first advertisement published in the New York Gazette in May 1777. It quickly gained popularity among American aristocrats, including prominent individuals such as George Washington and Thomas Jefferson.

Ice cream toppings enhance both the flavor and enjoyment of ice cream. Traditional favorites such as hot fudge and sprinkles, alongside more unconventional choices like candied bacon and exotic fruits, transform a basic scoop into a delightful indulgence. They offer endless possibilities for creative combinations, ensuring each scoop is unique and enjoyable.

FREEZE

Brain freeze, scientifically known as sphenopalatine ganglion neuralgia, happens when ice cream makes contact with the roof of your mouth. This interaction leads to the constriction and subsequent dilation of blood vessels, sending a rapid pain signal to the brain and causing a sudden headache.

Ice cream served as a morale booster for the U.S. military during World War I, quickly gaining popularity. By World War II, the military took it a step further by establishing small ice cream factories and even a floating ice cream barge to ensure that troops had access to this delightful treat.

In 2023, the USA went on a frosty spree, churning out a whopping 1.3 billion gallons of ice cream!

The earliest known ice cream flavor was savored by Alexander the Great around 2 B.C., consisting of a delightful combination of snow, ice, honey, and nectar.

Chocolate ice cream was developed before vanilla, with its origins tracing back to Italy in approximately 1693. In contrast, vanilla ice cream gained popularity later, in France during the 1760s.

#1

Vanilla ranks as the most popular ice cream flavor, celebrated for its simple yet indulgent taste.

The flavor that ranks as the second most popular ice cream choice is chocolate.

A rare ice cream flavor is garlic ice cream. It's known for its strong, unique taste and is often featured at California's annual Garlic Festival.

Cotton candy is like the sugary superstar of ice cream flavors, strutting its sweet stuff and making taste buds do a happy dance!

Strawberry ice cream boasts a fascinating history, with its roots dating back to at least 1813, when it was served at President James Madison's second inaugural banquet.

An earlier account from 1744 also mentions that Maryland Governor Thomas Bladen served a dessert of frozen strawberries and ice cream.

The reigning champ of ice cream toppings? Whipped cream, the fluffy superstar of sundaes!

The runner-up in the ice cream topping showdown? Hot fudge, ready to drizzle its chocolaty goodness!

Ben & Jerry's, born in 1978 thanks to the dynamic duo Ben Cohen and Jerry Greenfield in the charming town of Burlington, Vermont, is the rock star of the ice cream world with its wild and wacky flavors!

It's difficult to determine a precise figure. There are thousands of ice cream flavors around the globe, ranging from beloved classics such as vanilla and chocolate to one-of-a-kind and inventive options like everything bagel, honey lavender, and wasabi.

If you find yourself in Maryland during the summer, be sure to explore the Maryland Ice Cream Trail. This annual event showcases local creameries and features 12 dairies serving delicious, farm-fresh ice cream. Participants who visit all the locations can earn prizes, making it a wonderful opportunity for family fun and outdoor adventures.

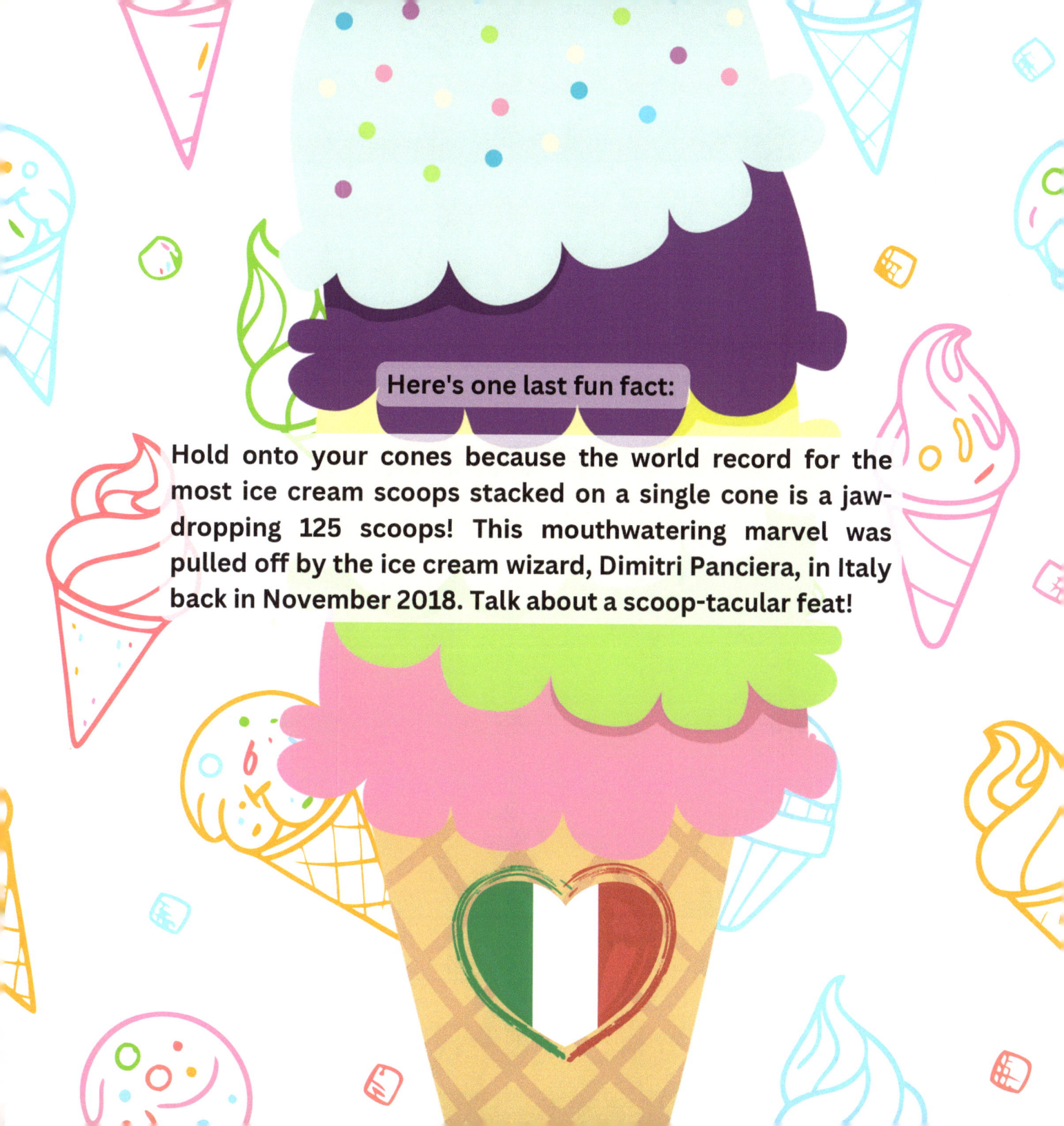

Here's one last fun fact:

Hold onto your cones because the world record for the most ice cream scoops stacked on a single cone is a jaw-dropping 125 scoops! This mouthwatering marvel was pulled off by the ice cream wizard, Dimitri Panciera, in Italy back in November 2018. Talk about a scoop-tacular feat!

The End!

Can you name the flavors?

Ice Cream Flavors

- Butter Pecan
- Cherry
- Chocolate
- Chocolate Chip
- Strawberry
- Mint Chocolate Chip
- Blue Moon
- Coconut
- Peach
- Batter

- Vanilla
- Coffee
- Banana
- Black Walnut
- Caramel Cone Crunch
- Brownie Batter
- Chocolate Peanut Butter
- Mango
- Rum Raisin
- Pumpkin

- Raspberry Ripple
- Blueberry
- Tutti Frutti
- Watermelon
- Superman
- Moon Mist
- Pistachio
- Earl Grey Tea
- Rainbow
- Sweet Potato

What other flavors have you eaten?

Ice Cream Toppings

- Hot Fudge
- Peanut Butter
- Whip Cream
- Caramel
- Butterscotch
- Marshmallow
- Cherries
- Sprinkles
- Chocolate Chips
- Walnuts

- Bananas
- Cherries
- Blueberries
- Strawberries
- Gummy Bears
- Cereal
- Coconut
- M&M's
- Cookie Dough
- Magic Shell

- Waffle Cone
- Watermelon
- Toasted Coconut
- Chocolate Bark
- Reese's
- Almonds
- Oreo Cookies
- Pretzels
- Raisins
- Brownies

- Strawberry Fluff
- Nutella
- Vanilla Wafers
- Whoppers
- Graham Crackers
- Jams
- Honey
- Granola
- Chocolate Raisins
- Skittles

www.ingramcontent.com/pod-product-compliance
Lightning Source LLC
Chambersburg PA
CBHW040028050426
42453CB00002B/48